Hermit Crab Care for Beginners

Everything You Need to Know About Raising Healthy, Happy Pet Hermit Crabs.

By

Jensen Kendall

ISBN-13: 978-1542668651
ISBN-10: 1542668654

Table of Contents

My First Experience With Hermit Crabs

I remember my first experience with Hermit Crabs like it was yesterday. It didn't involve my parents taking me to the pet store. My experience was a little different. My first experience with these little creatures came from a trip to the Florida Keys, a truly beautiful tropical oasis. We spent two weeks soaking up the sun, snorkeling with fish and mingling with the local animal population. Ah, the memories.

We spent our days on my dad's sailboat. We fished, sailed and snorkeled until the sun disappeared into the beautiful blue waters. When night came around, we ventured back to our campsite and slept in the tent. Some might say we were roughing it, but I would strongly disagree. There was nothing rough about this lifestyle. It was paradise.

There wasn't much to do at night. We could stare at the stars or soak a fishing line in hopes of a monster catch, but I preferred exploring the beach at night with my trusty flashlight. Why? Because that is when the Hermit Crabs emerged from their hiding places like an army of alien creatures.

The beach came to life with these shell toting crabs. A new world quickly made itself known to me. These Hermit Crabs were everywhere. There were little tiny ones that barely made a sound as their legs scratched the sand and there were huge ones that you could hear crawling on the beach, in the bushes and up the trees. They didn't seem to have a care in the world. They just went about their business. In fact, they seemed to have some sort of predefined destination in mind. They were so busy! I was amazed.

I quickly noticed each one had a different shell on its back. Why did this Hermit Crab pick this specific shell? Why did that Hermit Crab choose that shell? Was it the shape, the size or possibly the color? Did they favor one type of shell over another? My mind was full of questions but then I saw one Hermit Crab that really made me stop and wonder.

What was on that Hermit Crab's back? It wasn't a shell. I aimed my flashlight and took a few steps closer. The hermit crab got scared and hid inside its chosen home. At my feet was a plastic aspirin bottle and yes, this clever little Hermit Crab had decided to use that old empty aspirin bottle as a shell.

I had to hold it. I had to make sure this little crab was indeed carrying around an empty aspirin bottle. I reached down and picked it up. I slowly turned the bottle over and peered inside the opening. There were little purple legs and one large pincer carefully curled up in the bottom of the plastic bottle. I couldn't believe what I was seeing. I laughed and gently placed the Hermit Crab back on that long stretch of beach and watched as the aspirin bottle sprouted legs and slowly disappeared into the night.

This was my first experience with these fascinating creatures and it wouldn't be until many years later that I owned one as a pet. Well, actually I bought one for my son who would wind up naming his Hermit Crab "Purple Pincher." Little did we know that this was the actual name of the specific species we had purchased!

Why Choose Hermit Crabs?

If you haven't already asked yourself this very important question, you should. While Hermit Crabs are very easy to care for, they are living creatures that DO NEED a very specific environment in order to survive. If you can't supply this type of environment, then your Hermit Crabs won't be happy and they will most likely die. I'm not trying to deter you from owning a few of these awesome little creatures. I just want to make sure you fully understand what you are getting into. Let's take a closer look at the pros and cons of owning Hermit Crabs. You might be surprised to learn why these creatures make such great pets!

Hermit Crabs Don't Smell!

Most pets, be it the family dog or the sly old cat will eventually be the cause of some sort of foul smell. It could be regular gas, pooping in the wrong place or some stink that just seems to come from their coat. With Hermit Crabs you will never have a problem of odor from the Hermit Crabs themselves. They are odorless, at least to humans.

While the Hermit Crabs themselves might not have an odor, their habitat will develop an odor if it is not properly taken care of. This of course is up to you. Your little Hermit Crabs aren't going to be doing much cleaning in their habitat and I don't know of any Hermit Crab maid services. Yes, you will be required to do some routine habitat maintenance, but the amount of work involved is very small. That brings us to the next point.

Hermit Crabs Need Little to No Maintenance!

Hermit Crabs are truly unique and over time you will notice each one has its very own personality. You will also notice that the Hermit Crabs themselves require little to no maintenance. Keeping up with the habitat is another story. You will need to do a little bit of work to keep their environment in good shape but we are talking mere minutes a day if that. The trade-off is well worth the effort.

Hermit Crabs Take Up Very Little Space!

Yet another reason Hermit Crabs make excellent pets. They don't need a whole lot of space. Your average 10 gallon or 37.85 Liter aquarium will provide plenty of space for your new Hermit Crabs. The average size of a 10 gallon aquarium is only 20 inches by 20 inches by 12 inches or 50 centimeters by 50 centimeters by 30 centimeters. A 10 gallon aquarium would have no problems fitting on top of your average dresser, night stand or end table.

Hermit Crabs Are Cheap!

Hermit Crabs are inexpensive on every level. Not only are the crabs themselves affordable but you can buy everything you need to keep them happy and healthy for around $100.00. That is by far one of the smallest price tags you will find for owning a pet.

No Expensive Trips to the Vet!

While we are on the topic of expenses, you will be happy to know that Hermit Crabs will not require regular trips to the veterinarian's office. You also won't have to shell out cash for yearly vaccinations like you would with most furry four legged friends.

Hermit Crabs Are Not Destructive!

Dogs love to chew on things. These things often include your favorite shoes, a purse and sometimes the couch. Cats are known to be equally destructive with their claws. The good news about Hermit Crabs in this regard is the simple fact that they won't be destroying any of these things!

Hermit Crabs Won't Poop on the Floor!

This benefit is pretty simple. You won't be coming home to any surprise messes on the floor.

Hermit Crabs Won't Trigger Allergies!

Luckily I am not allergic to cats or dogs. If you do have common pet allergies you will be happy to know that Hermit Crabs won't be a problem.

No Shedding!

Cats and dogs both shed quite a bit of hair. I love my dogs but I don't love the huge piles of hair that seem to appear overnight.

Hermit Crabs Are Mostly Quiet!
If you live in a small apartment where noise from pets might be an issue, you won't have any problems with Hermit Crabs because they are mostly quiet. Notice how I said "mostly." Hermit Crabs are nocturnal creatures. This means they are most active at night when you are most likely trying to sleep. You will be surprised at just how much noise these little creatures make at night in their habitat. If you are light sleeper, don't keep your Hermit Crabs in your bedroom.

Those are all the reasons why Hermit Crabs make excellent pets. Here are a few reasons you might not want to own a group of Hermit Crabs.

Don't Expect Hermit Crabs to Cuddle
If you are looking for a pet that will enjoy snuggling with you on the couch, Hermit Crabs are not the right choice. Hermit Crabs are very social creatures but they prefer to be social with their own kind. I'm not saying that you can't handle them because you most definitely should. Just don't expect any warm cuddling!

Hermit Crabs Can Live A Long Time!
There is a very common misconception about the lifespan of a Hermit Crab. If you create a good environment for these little creatures, they will live a long time. How long? Some species can live well over 25 years. Don't think that owning Hermit Crabs will be a short venture. You can expect years of fun with these little creatures.

Hermit Crab Habitats Require Regular Maintenance
If you are looking for a 100% maintenance free pet, Hermit Crabs might not be the best choice. I have already said that the Hermit Crabs themselves require little to no maintenance, but their habitats do. It only takes a few minutes a day to make sure their habitat is perfect.

Humidity Levels Are Crucial for Survival!
Part of the routine maintenance you will be doing is maintaining proper humidity levels. Please don't ignore this simple fact. If the humidity level in your Hermit Crab habitat is not correct, your Hermit Crabs will die. This is a simple fact.

Hermit Crabs have gills, even the land dwelling variety. This means they need moisture in order to breathe. If your Hermit Crab habitat has little to no humidity, your Hermit Crabs will suffocate. Don't worry though, I will show you how to keep humidity levels where they should be. It is very easy and very inexpensive.

Hermit Crabs Need Chlorine Free Water
Unfortunately most of the tap water we drink has been treated with Chlorine. The chlorine will burn their gills and cause problems. Using tap water will slowly kill your Hermit Crabs. This may seem like a rather large problem, but it is not.

You can buy inexpensive water conditioners at almost every major pet store or online. Some of the more popular brands include:

- API Tap Water Conditioner
- API Stress Coat Water Conditioner
- Tetra Aquasafe

This stuff is very inexpensive and lasts quite a while.

That's it! As you can see, owning Hermit Crabs is pretty simple. You won't have half the problems of a traditional four legged pet.

Do Hermit Crabs Make Good Pets for Kids?

As an adult it can be very satisfying watching your children learn important lessons from the animal world and the right pet can help create wonderful memories. It can also teach children the true value of responsibility. The right pet can be a win win situation for every living creature involved, but what about Hermit Crabs? Do they make good pets for kids?

Hermit Crabs can be an excellent first pet for children. Just remember that they are living creatures with a pretty long lifespan. Your children will have to keep their new friends for as long as ten years and we all know children tire of things very quickly. Parents often get stuck with pets children grow tired of. This could be you?

Hermit Crabs are fun and easy to take care of. We have already established that but it can be difficult to remember what it was like to be a kid. Your children will have to be taught how to interact with their new friends. I never even considered that I would be spending more time teaching my son how to properly handle, care for and respect his Hermit Crabs than watching the Hermit Crabs, but that is exactly what happened.

If you as a parent have a positive attitude towards the new Hermit Crabs, you can bet your kids will as well. Excitement is contagious and makes for a good example. The same could be said about having a negative attitude towards these little creatures.

You will also be responsible for teaching your children how to care for their new friends. Which means you will have to invest some quality time into the crabs and your children. I told you owning Hermit Crabs can be a win win situation for every living creature involved.

With all that said, there are a few precautions that should be taken with children and Hermit Crabs. I know I have already said this, but it is a very important fact to consider. Hermit Crabs are not cuddly creatures that want to sit in your child's lap. They are very busy creatures who would prefer to spend their time moving things around in their habitat.

Hermit Crabs can and sometimes will pinch.
I would love to say that it doesn't hurt when this happens, but it does hurt and a single pinch might be enough to prevent your children from wanting to spend time with their new friends. A quick pinch could also cause your child to drop the Hermit Crab on the floor or throw them across the room as a reflex. I shouldn't have to tell you this, but dropping or throwing a Hermit Crab will most likely kill it.

Hermit Crabs will usually only pinch if they are scared or if they feel like they are going to fall but there is always one or two in a group who just seem grumpy.

The worst part about getting pinched is waiting for the Hermit Crab to let go. Sometimes it can take as long as ten minutes. If you find a Hermit Crab has decided to hold on with a pincer, the best thing to do is place your hand back in their habitat and they will usually let go.

Holding your palm flat will often prevent a pinch or you could always put a soft sock on your hand to protect it.

Hermit Crabs Species

You may have noticed how I keep mentioning Hermit Crabs in the plural form. Don't buy just one. Owning just one crab isn't the best idea. These little creatures love to be social and they need some companionship. Two is better but three should be perfect.

Don't worry about the extra Hermit Crabs inflating your costs either because they won't. In fact, the actual Hermit Crabs are going to be the least expensive part of the entire cost equation here. Your habitat needs won't be any greater either. You can easily house three good sized Hermit Crabs in one ten gallon aquarium. Remember, more is better in this situation!

You should also know that your new Hermit Crabs should be land dwellers. Hermit Crabs that actually live in the water will require much more to survive including a saltwater aquarium setup. Saltwater aquariums don't come cheap and setting up a saltwater tank is far beyond the scope of this book.

Now that you know you will most likely be owning more than one of these interesting little crabs, let's take a closer look at the different species.

Purple Pincher Hermit Crabs
This is by far the most common type of Hermit Crab on the market today. There is a really good chance that your crabs will be Purple pinchers and that is a good thing because they are very easy to care for. They make great pets and they have a very interesting social life. You will find yourself spending hours watching them go about their nightly routines. Some people, myself included fall in love with their beautiful colors. The Purple Pincher is also known as the Caribbean Crab because that is where they are naturally found.

The overall temperament of the Purple Pincher is very good and they are a little slower than most species. They get along great with people and of course they like to be around more of their own kind but they have been known to fight over shells. If a Purple Pincher sees another in a shell it likes, it will grab the shell and rock it back and forth until the defending crab abandons it. Sometimes the crab defending its shell will make a loud chirp noise. These skirmishes are rarely a problem but they can turn deadly.

Ecuadorian Hermit Crab
The Ecuadorian Hermit Crab is one of the smallest Hermit Crabs on the market and they are known to be very fast! You would be surprised at how quick these little crabs can move.

They will often prefer to use a smaller shell that might look as if it won't fit. Using a smaller shell allows them to move more quickly. Ecuadorian Hermit Crabs would prefer to run away where as a Purple Pincher might be more apt to close up and hide inside its shell.

The colors of this species varies. They can be green, orange, bright blue, yellow, tan or orange. These colors will change as the crab grows and molts. You will also notice that these Hermit Crabs are very busy. They are always doing something even during daylight hours and they will often communicate with each other by chirping.

Ecuadorian Hermit Crabs are often very skittish around people and some of them have been known to be aggressive. They are also known for creating deep tunnels and climbing anything in their habitat.

Because they are so fast and such good climbers, it is very important to make sure your habitat is secure. They have been known to escape.

These are the two most common types of Hermit Crabs found in the pet industry. There are a few other species that are starting to show up as well.

Strawberry Hermit Crabs
Can you guess why this species of Hermit Crab is called "Strawberry?" Could it be their vibrant red color? Well, of course! You will also find some that have more of an orange tint to them. Strawberry Hermit Crabs are also the only land species to have what is referred to as an "opalescent" sheen. Their exoskeletons appear to show multiple colors at different angles.

Strawberries are one of the most active Hermit Crab species and will spend most of their time moving about their habitat. They love to dig and require a good amount of substrate depth in order to be happy. Strawberries are also known to be somewhat fragile and difficult to care for.

Blueberry Hermit Crabs
Yet another Hermit Crab aptly named for its beautiful colors. If you guessed that these Hermit Crabs are more of a blue color, you would be 100% correct. This species of Hermit Crab is rarely seen in pet stores.

Aussie Hermit Crabs
The native Australian Hermit Crab is most likely only going to be found in Australia. Who would have thought? They vary widely in color but are most often white or brown. Good on ya mate!

Ruggie Hermit Crabs
Last but definitely not least, we have the Ruggie Hermit Crabs. These Hermit Crabs are also a little on the rare side. You will most likely only find them on the Internet. They vary widely in color and are known to be very mellow crabs. These Hermit Crabs are not recommended for first time crab keepers.

Now that you know a little more information about the various species of Hermit Crabs, let's take a closer look at actually buying and choosing your first Hermit Crabs.

Choosing the Perfect Hermit Crabs

You basically have only two choices when it comes to purchasing your new Hermit Crabs. You can purchase them online or you can pay a visit to your local pet store and see what is in stock. Some people might think about scouring the beach and collecting a few Hermit Crabs from the wild. Don't do this! Not only is this a bad idea, it is illegal in some locations.

Should You Purchase Your Hermit Crabs Online?
Purchasing any type of pet online can be a little tricky for several reasons.

1. You will be paying more for high shipping charges. Shipping any type of live animal is going to be expensive.
2. Animals, including Hermit Crabs tend to get very stressed when shipped. In some cases, they die.
3. You have no way of knowing the condition of the Hermit Crabs before shipment. This is not good!

There is really only one positive reason for ordering Hermit Crabs online and that one reason is getting a better selection. Online vendors will have more exotic crabs in stock. This might be the only way to obtain certain species.

If you have chosen to avoid the online Hermit Crab market - (A really good idea) - then you only have one option left. You will need to take a trip to your local pet store. Here is what you need to pay close attention to once you arrive!

Take a look at the overall condition of the entire pet store. The first bad clue is usually a foul smell. Pet stores that don't properly clean animal habitats will smell like urine or feces. If your pet store smells like this, you may want to choose another one.

If the pet store passes "The Smell Test," then you should take a look at all of the animals in the store, not just the Hermit Crabs. Again, just use your best judgment to determine whether or not the pet store is properly taking care of their animals.

Look at all the habitats. Do they appear clean? Is there fresh food and water? Do the animals look happy and healthy? These are all very important questions you should be asking yourself before you approach the Hermit Crabs. Once you locate the crabs, here's what you should be looking for.

Active Crabs are Healthy Crabs!
The first sign of a healthy Hermit Crab is an active Hermit Crab, but this can tricky to determine. Hermit Crabs are nocturnal and most pet stores are closed at night so the Hermit Crabs will most likely be sleeping. This makes it difficult to determine if a crab is actually healthy or not.

You might need to wake the crab up. This can be done by picking up the Hermit Crab. Most Hermit Crabs are very curious. Once you pick them up, they will want to see what is going on.

Avoid Hermit Crabs With Painted Shells!
Painted shells might look cute but they can be extremely toxic. Hermit Crabs like to eat just about anything they can get a hold of, this includes the chipping paint on a painted shell. Most paints have enough toxic materials to kill a Hermit Crab with just a little nibble.

Don't Choose Hermit Crabs Without Shells!
Hermit Crabs rarely leave their shells. In fact, their shells are their only line of defense. A Hermit Crab that chooses to walk around without a shell is not well.

Avoid Crabs With Mites!
Some Hermit Crabs attract mites. These little pests will eventually kill a Hermit Crab. These mites are tiny and very difficult to see but they **DO NOT** like direct sunlight. If you can take your Hermit Crab choices out into the sunshine, you will be able to see the mites scatter.

Hermit Crab Habitats Must Be Free of Other Animals and Insects!

There should be no animals of any type in the Hermit Crab habitat. If your pet store is putting other animals in with their Hermit Crabs, then you need to start shopping somewhere else. If there are any signs of insects in the habitat, then you should also start looking elsewhere for your new friends.

Okay, now that you know all of the potential problems to avoid, how do you actually pick the perfect Hermit Crabs? This is the easy part.

Choose Different Sized Hermit Crabs!

I already talked a little about Hermit Crabs fighting, choosing different sized Hermit Crabs will help prevent this. If all of the Hermit Crabs have different sized shells, there will not be much fighting.

Make Sure Your Hermit Crabs Are All Going to Get Along!

Some Hermit Crabs just don't get along and it has nothing to do with shells. Some of them are just grumpy. When you think you have chosen all of your new Hermit Crabs, put them all in a container together. If one of them appears to be aggressive, replace it with another.

That's all there is to it, but what makes the perfect Hermit Crab habitat? Let's find out.

What Makes the Perfect Hermit Crab Habitat?

Now for the fun part. Getting all of the supplies needed to make the perfect Hermit Crab habitat is just the beginning of the fun. The real fun comes when you start setting up the habitat. Not only do you get to create the entire habitat, but you also get to decorate it. I personally love this part of the process. It gives me the opportunity to create the perfect little ecosystem for my crabs. Let's get to it.

Most pet stores will at least attempt to help you purchase everything you need in order to make your Hermit Crabs happy and healthy. You can't really blame them for this because it is how they make their money. Pet stores make far more profit on all of the accessories you will need to buy, but most pet store employees will often recommend the **WRONG** items for your new Hermit Crab habitat.

Hermit Crabs have very specific needs that a lot of pet store employees are unaware of. I'm not trying to belittle pet store employees, no way. The vast majority of them work in the pet trade because they truly do love the animals they sell, but if you want your Hermit Crabs to live a long healthy life, here is what you need to do.

Avoid Hermit Crab Kits Online

I have seen plenty of larger online vendors selling "Hermit Crab Kits." This sounds like a great idea, but most of these kits are very, very wrong in so many ways. Don't waste your time purchasing an online Hermit Crab habitat kit. Here are the items you will need to make your Hermit Crabs happy and healthy.

The Hermit Crab Habitat Basics

Aquarium – The first and most important item you will need is the **GLASS** aquarium. Do not buy one of those little plastic pet containers for your main Hermit Crab habitat. A 10 gallon glass aquarium makes the perfect base for your new habitat.

Isolation Container

An isolation container is also a really good idea to have on hand. If you have the space, an additional 10 gallon glass aquarium will work perfectly. If you are short on space, you can use one of the small plastic pet containers sold at pet stores but remember, this is only for isolating a Hermit Crab. Why would you want to isolate one of your Hermit Crabs? I'll cover that topic a little later in the book.

Screen Lid – You will most definitely need a secure screen lid for your new habitat. Most species of Hermit Crabs love to climb and some of them have even managed to magically climb the corners of an aquarium.

A secure screen lid will help keep your Hermit Crabs in their new home and provide some much needed fresh air. It will also help keep other animals out of the habitat. You can easily secure the lid with a few small pieces of tape that don't cover any part of the screen. You don't want your Hermit Crabs eating the glue on the tape. Make sure the tape only touches the outside of the aquarium and a small portion of the screen lid.

Substrate

You will need something to line the bottom of your Hermit Crab habitat. Hermit Crabs like to dig. Choosing the wrong type of substrate is a very common mistake.

Bad Substrate Choices

- **Gravel** – Cheap and easily found, gravel should be avoided. Hermit Crabs can't dig in gravel and most gravel is dyed to make it look more visually appealing.
- **Calcium Sand** – Even though this product is called "sand," it is not. Calcium sand is made from calcium carbonate. This is the same stuff you find in chalk and antacids. Most calcium sand is dyed and it is supposed to be kept dry. Your Hermit Crab habitat needs humidity. How can you keep the environment humid if the substrate needs to be dry? You can't. Calcium sand and water equals mold! You don't want mold in your habitat.
- **Reptile Sand** – Reptile Sand is much like Calcium Sand. In fact, the two are often interchangeable. This substrate is for reptiles that require a dry environment. Water mixed with Reptile Sand encourages mold growth.
- **Live Sand** – Live sand is great in saltwater fish tanks. It helps create a stable ecosystem because it is full of bacteria that is needed to create a healthy saltwater environment. This bacteria can be very dangerous to land dwelling Hermit Crabs. Don't use it.
- **Wood Chips** – This is quite possibly the single worst choice for Hermit Crab habitat substrate. Don't even consider it.

Good Substrate Choices

- **Coconut Fiber** – This is by far the best choice for a substrate. Coconut fiber resists mold and can help keep your habitat at the perfect humidity level. Hermit Crabs are naturally found in tropical environments where coconut fiber is often found. Giving them exactly what is found in nature is always the best choice. Just be careful with the compressed coconut fiber because it will expand quite a bit.

- **Play Sand** – Play sand also makes an excellent substrate choice for your new Hermit Crab habitat. You can often find this stuff at major home improvement stores like Lowe's and Home Depot. Play sand is great, but try to avoid play sand that is specifically for children. It will work, but Play Sand that is labeled for landscaping works the best.
- **Beach Sand** – Providing exactly what is found in nature is a great idea so you would think sand from the local beach would make the perfect substrate and it might, but regular old beach sand might introduce some unwanted pests, bacteria and other problems.

The Best Substrate Choice?

The best substrate choice is a combination of coconut fiber and play sand. This has proven to be a winning combination that fights mold growth while keeping enough moisture to maintain a healthy humidity level! How much should you use? That all depends on the Hermit Crab species. Don't worry, I will cover that topic a little later in this book.

All right, now we are making some progress. You should have the perfect housing and the perfect substrate, but what else are you going to need in order to keep your Hermit Crabs happy and healthy?

Food and Water Bowls

The only real issue you will have with choosing food and water dishes is depth. You don't want dishes that are too deep, especially when it comes to water. If your Hermit Crabs can't easily get out of their water dishes, they will drown. Make sure they are shallow.

It is also a good idea to put a small natural sea sponge in the water bowl. Not only will this help keep humidity levels where they should be, but it will also give your Hermit Crabs a way to climb out. Just be careful using a sponge because they can introduce mold.

I prefer to use shallow natural sea shells for dishes. They are not too deep and they help make the habitat look a little more tropical!

Don't make the mistake of getting only two bowls, one for water and one for food. You will need at least **THREE BOWLS**.

- Food Bowl
- Fresh water bowl
- Salt water bowl

Your new Hermit Crabs will need both a fresh water dish and a salt water dish. Don't try to make your salt water dish using ordinary table salt either! I will go over the proper way to prepare salt water for your Hermit Crabs a little later in this book.

Keeping Your Hermit Crab Habitat the Right Temperature

If you don't happen to live in a warmer climate, then you will need to make sure the temperature in your Hermit Crab habitat is warm enough. Remember, Hermit Crabs are naturally found in tropical environments where temperatures are a little on the warm side. This means you have to keep your new habitat at the proper temperature. The perfect temperature is somewhere around 70-75 degrees Fahrenheit or 21 to 23 degrees Celsius.

How do you go about keeping the habitat at the perfect temperature?
The easiest solution is by using a heating pad designed specifically for reptiles. Your local pet store should be able to help you with this. These heating pads are placed under the habitat and are an excellent choice for maintaining temperatures.

DO NOT PURCHASE A HEAT ROCK!

Your local pet store may suggest purchasing a heat rock for your new Hermit Crab habitat. Don't. Heat rocks get far too hot for Hermit Crabs. A heat rock can very easily burn your new little friends.

Habitat Lighting

You will also be responsible for regulating the lighting in your new Hermit Crab habitat. Some Hermit Crab owners prefer a heat lamp. While this sounds like a great idea to help maintain proper temperatures, it can be problematic. If a heat lamp is placed too close to the Hermit Crabs, bad things will happen. You don't want to cook your new crabs. They just need to stay warm.

For lighting that provides no heat, try Florescent bulbs and white LEDS.

Heat lamps are okay if they are kept far enough away and are only used during the day. You have to maintain a normal day – night cycle in your Hermit Crab habitat. Keeping a heat lamp on all night will make this impossible!

Which brings us to the next point, night lighting. Hermit Crabs are nocturnal. They are most active at night. You will be pleasantly surprised at just how active these little creatures get once the sun goes down. They love to spend the evening rearranging everything in their habitat. This is the best time to pull up a chair and watch your crabs go about their nightly routines but a normal, bright light might send them running for cover and interrupt the important day-night cycle they need.

Some pet store sell what is called a "moon light." These lights are perfect for watching your little Hermit Crabs. You can also go with a red or blue LED lamp for nighttime viewing.

Keeping Track of Heat and Humidity

I know I have already said this, but I am going to say it again. Your Hermit Crabs need a very specific temperature and humidity level in order to live happy, healthy lives. You can't provide this perfect environment if you can't determine things like temperature and humidity levels. This is where a little bit of science mixed with modern technology provides you with the perfect solution: a temperature / humidity gauge.

You could buy a separate temperature and a separate humidity gauge but why bother when you can pick up one product that will tell you what both of these are with a simple glance? You can find one of these at your local pet store or online. The Zoo Med brand appears to be the most popular.

Having this handy gauge is only half of the solution. You will also need to know what the temperature should be as well as the humidity levels.

- **The temperature should be 70-75 degrees Fahrenheit or 21 to 23 degrees Celsius.**
- **The humidity level should be 75-80%.**

Your new handy, dandy gauge will help you monitor both of these!

Hiding and Climbing Accessories

Hermit Crabs need a nice place to hide during the day. This will help them maintain the important day – night cycle. Your local pet store should be able to help you with a Hermit Crab hide out. If you can't find one locally, there are plenty of great choices on the Internet. Make sure to get one that is big enough for all of your Hermit Crabs because they love to huddle together when they are sleeping.

You will also need to give them something to climb. They love to explore and providing some climbing material will help them get the exercise they need. **Cholla wood** makes a good choice because it is naturally resistant to mold and rot. It is a dried cactus skeleton. The only problem is finding the stuff. If you happen to live in the southwest United States, then you won't have any problems. Otherwise, you can find it pretty easily online.

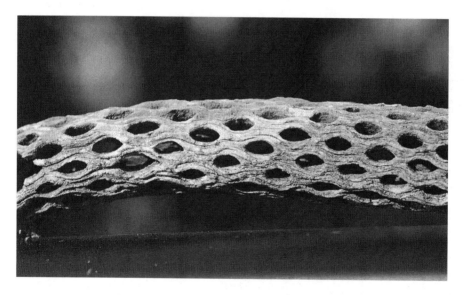

Your local pet store should also be able to provide you some good climbing materials. Look for a coconut fiber climbing wall. It makes an excellent choice. Just make sure the climbing material you choose is not: plastic, painted or dyed.

Driftwood sounds like a good idea, but you never know where it is coming from or more importantly, where it has been. It could be loaded with all sorts of nasty things that are harmful to your Hermit Crabs.

Extra Shells are Vital!

Hermit Crabs don't actually make their own shells. They use empty shells they find on the beach and this shell is the only thing that protects the Hermit Crab from the outside world. Without a shell, a Hermit Crab would surely die. This means that you will need to purchase a few extra shells.

A good general rule is to have at least three empty shells for each Hermit Crab you purchase. This will provide them with plenty of opportunities to make sure they are carrying around the best shell, but you can't use any shell. Hermit Crabs have very specific tastes when it comes to the home they wear on their backs. Before you purchase some extra shells, here are two very important things to remember.

DON'T BUY SHELLS THAT HAVE BEEN PAINTED.

NEVER TRY TO REMOVE A HERMIT CRAB FROM ITS SHELL.

With that out of the way, here is everything you need to know about picking up some extra shells for your new little friends.

Choosing extra shells is really a lot of fun. Not only will your Hermit Crabs be very happy, but having all the extra shells laying around in the habitat will make it look more tropical. Thankfully you can easily find plenty of extra shells online at places like Etsy, Ebay and even Amazon.

Are Some Shells A Better Choice Than Others?
The quick and simple answer is, YES! Certain Hermit Crab species will always seem to prefer certain types of shells. This is because certain types of shells are a much better fit for certain types of Hermit Crabs.

The Purple Pincher or Caribbean Hermit Crab seems to prefer a shell that comes from a species of sea snails called Turbo Snails. These shells have a silky smooth interior that feels cool and smooth to a Hermit Crab. It is almost like wearing silk! Purple pincers have also been known to like Tiger Snail shells as well. Both of these shells feature a nice round opening which makes a perfect fit for the Purple Pincher Hermit Crab.

If you have Ecuadorian Hermit Crabs, you will need a different type of shell. This species of Hermit Crab prefers a shell with an opening which has more of a stretched oval or slotted shape.

Does Size Matter?
This is one area where size does play a very important role. The whole reason you are purchasing extra shells is because your Hermit Crabs will outgrow their current shells. If you pick a bunch of shells that are too small, then your Hermit Crabs won't fit. The same could be said of choosing shells that are too large. This means you have to choose shells that are the perfect size. Don't worry, it is a lot easier than it sounds and a handful of extra shells will only cost a few dollars.

You should be choosing shells that are just a little larger than the shells your Hermit Crabs are currently using. The most important part in relation to "size," is the actual shell opening. Choose shells that have a slightly larger opening. Typically a shell that has an opening around ¼ of inch larger should be fine.

Hermit Crabs are funny when it comes to choosing a new shell. Some Hermit Crabs will get very excited when they see new shells and change quite frequently only to wind up sticking with the shell they were originally using. Other Hermit Crabs will be very picky about their shells and each Hermit Crab does seem to have a specific style of shell they prefer. Each Hermit Crab is different and that is part of the fun!

Where Should You Buy Extra Shells?

Your local pet store may have plenty of extra shells on hand. If they do not have a decent supply, you can easily find plenty of replacement shells online. I have found the best prices on Etsy.com. Just try searching for "hermit crab shells," or "turbo tapestry shells." The only problem with shopping for extra shells online is the simple fact that you can't easily determine their exact size.

Is There Anything Special That Needs to Be Done to the Extra Shells?

It is always a very good idea to give the extra shells a very good cleaning and the best way to do this is by boiling them for at least five minutes. This will kill any bacteria, mold or other living creatures that may have taken up residence in the shells. Make sure you let the shells cool for at least an hour before placing them in your Hermit Crab habitat. Pull up a chair and watch the Hermit Crab moving party begin!

Setting Up the Perfect Hermit Crab Habitat

Now that you have everything you need to setup the perfect Hermit Crab habitat, it is time to get to work setting things up the right way. This is the fun part. You get to create a cool little world for your Hermit Crabs to enjoy. Let's start with proper placement.

Proper Placement
There are a few things to consider when you are ready to setup your new habitat. Before you put anything inside the habitat, think about where you are going to put it. There might be a few areas in your home that will only make it difficult for you to maintain proper temperature and humidity levels.

1. Avoid placing the habitat directly under or over air conditioning and heating vents.
2. Avoid placing the habitat in direct sunlight.

You should also think about other pets when choosing the perfect place to put the habitat. Dogs will definitely want to sniff out the entire habitat. While this generally isn't going to be a problem, make sure your dogs can't easily knock the habitat over.

Cats on the other hand can cause problems. If you are a cat lover, then you know just how curious they can be. You most likely also know that movement of practically any type will really increase the curiosity levels of a cat. This is just one more reason why a secured screen lid should is a great choice. You don't want your cat getting inside the Hermit Crab habitat. While most cats are only curious, some cats are also a little on the devious side. As a cat lover, I'm sure you are well aware of this. Think about your cat before you decide to setup your Hermit Crab habitat.

Substrate Levels

Once you have chosen the perfect place to put your Hermit Crab habitat, it is time to start setting things up. The first piece to the puzzle is making sure you have the proper amount of substrate in the bottom of the habitat. It is also a very good idea to make sure whatever you have chosen to put the habitat on can safely support the weight. If you have chosen a 10 gallon aquarium for your habitat, the finished setup weight can be as much as 40 pounds. No one wants to wake up in the middle of the night to the sound of a Hermit Crab habitat falling to the ground. It could be even worse waking up to a Hermit Crab crawling across your face!

A general rule is to have enough substrate in the bottom of your habitat so your largest Hermit Crab can be completely buried. In most cases, filling your habitat halfway works great. It may seem like too much, but it is not. Some Hermit Crabs not only enjoy digging, burrowing and tunneling but there are times when they actually need to do this.

If you chose to go with a mixture of coconut fiber and play sand like I suggested, then you should mix them at a ratio of 5:1. Five parts sand to every one part coconut fiber. Mix the two together and add them to your habitat.

If you are feeling a little bold, you can try a little sculpting with your new terrain. Some people will make hills, valleys and small areas for water. This is completely up to you, but it doing this adds to the fun of setting up the habitat. Your Hermit Crabs will appreciate your extra efforts as well.

If you are not the greatest at decorating, then just look online for some Hermit Crab habitat examples. You can just search Google for, "Hermit Crab Habitat" and look under images. You should see plenty of really cool habitats that might give you a little bit of inspiration.

Once you are satisfied with the substrate levels and overall layout of the habitat, start adding all of the other accessories.

- Hermit Crab Hideout
- Climbing Accessories
- Food and water dishes

What About A Moss Pit?
If you are feeling really adventurous, you can section off a small area of the habitat and create a moss pit. Hermit Crabs love these for several reasons.

1. Hermit Crabs love hiding in moss!
2. Hermit Crabs will often snack on moss!
3. Moss can help keep humidity levels in check!

Moss pits are great, **BUT SOME TYPES OF MOSS ARE POSIONOUS TO HERMIT CRABS.** If you want to make a moss pit, then use: **Sphagnum Moss.** This type of moss is safe for Hermit Crabs and can be easily found in most pet stores. If you can't find any at your local pet store, then try Amazon. I highly recommend ZooMed Sphagnum moss.

You can dig out a small area in your Habitat and line the spot with moss. Some people use small plastic containers for their moss pit. Get creative and have fun!

Feeding Your Hermit Crab Army

Feeding your Hermit Crab army is a lot of fun and it is really easy too. I have always enjoyed watching as my Hermit Crabs take notice of their fresh food. It is comical to watch them slowly approach the food and test it before devouring it all. It always makes me smile.

The greatest thing about feeding your Hermit Crabs is the huge variety of really great food you can give them. Let's start in the produce department because Hermit Crabs simply love fresh fruit and veggies. Organic will be your best choice and don't forget to wash the fruit and veggies before giving them to your Hermit Crabs! You can't go wrong with any of these!

Carrots – Hermit Crabs love carrots and the beta-carotene will help the Hermit Crabs keep their amazing colors. Shredded carrots work best.

Corn – Hermit Crabs love corn but a lot of the corn on the market today is GMO or genetically modified. I avoid it all together.

Broccoli – Of course broccoli crowns are the best. Try to avoid the frozen stuff. Fresh is always best.

Spinach – My Hermit Crabs seem to enjoy the tender baby spinach the most. It is fun to watch them pull little pieces off with their pincers.

Lettuce – Try to avoid the cheapo Iceburg Lettuce. It has no nutritional value. Green leaf or Romaine lettuce both make great choices.

Green Beans – I will give them both the shells and the beans. They seem to like them equally.

Sweet Potatoes – Another favorite and a great source of beta-carotene.

Cabbage – Not my favorite, but my Hermit Crabs enjoy it.

Coconut – You can't go wrong with coconut. Hermit Crabs eat this in the wild. Just make sure it isn't sweetened.

Mango – This is another favorite that Hermit Crabs find in the wild.

Grapes – My Hermit Crabs will only eat peeled grapes. Yes, I think my Hermit Crabs are a little spoiled.

Apple Slices - Organic and washed.

Banana – One of my favorites and my Hermit Crabs seem to really like them too!

Peaches – Again, peeled is best.

As you can see, you have plenty of great choices when it comes to fruits and veggies, but hermit Crabs are not vegetarians. They also enjoy eating certain types of meats as well. Much like us, Hermit Crabs need a properly balanced diet. Here are some meats your new Hermit Crabs will love. Just make sure there is no seasoning and don't give them anything raw.

Chicken - Small pieces of shredded chicken breast work best.

Fish – Of course Hermit Crabs love fish. It is something they often find in their natural habitat.

Shrimp – You can't go wrong with any type of shrimp either. My Hermit Crabs seem to really enjoy fresh steamed shrimp tails cut into tiny pieces.

Hermit Crabs also love nuts and grains as well. They are not very picky eaters.

Peanut Butter – Go with the organic stuff. Non-organic peanut butter has far too much garbage in it. My Hermit Crabs love this stuff. It gives them plenty of energy too!

Almonds, walnuts and peanuts – Don't get any special flavors and make sure they are not salted.

Plain oatmeal – Plain oatmeal is inexpensive and Hermit Crabs love it. Don't get instant oatmeal. Only use the good old fashioned stuff.

Rice – Just like oatmeal, plain non-instant rice is best. Mine prefer cooked plain rice.

What About "Hermit Crab" food?

Pet stores do sell a special type of food labeled, "Hermit Crab Food." I don't recommend this stuff for several reasons. It is always best to give your crabs fresh food. The store bought food is not fresh and in many cases it is full of junk. You don't need it.

Hermit Crabs have quite the palate and they will gladly eat any of the items mentioned above. Don't make the mistake of going out and buying everything listed here because Hermit Crabs aren't huge eaters. Which brings us to the all too important question.

How Much Should I Feed My Hermit Crabs?

I would love to tell you that there is a magical formula for determining just how much your Hermit Crabs will eat, but there isn't. But don't worry because figuring out their appetites is pretty simple. Give them a good amount of food and see how much they eat. Within a few days you will know exactly how much food to give your Hermit Crabs every evening.

Notice how I said, "evening" there? You should be feeding your Hermit Crabs their fresh assortment of food anywhere from 4:00 – 6:00 P.M. This is when they will start waking up looking for their breakfast. They will need plenty of energy for the night ahead.

Try to keep an eye out for hoarders. Some Hermit Crabs and this isn't species specific; like to hide food. You may or may not own a hoarding Hermit Crab but they do exist. Some will take their favorite foods and bury them in the substrate where they often forget about them.

A few days goes by and you start to wonder what that awful smell is coming from your Hermit Crab habitat. It is the hidden food which is now most likely ripe and moldy! Keep your eyes open for hoarders. They will be the single largest cause of a mold outbreak in your habitat.

You should be removing any uneaten food every morning and cleaning the food bowls. I have found that a nice soak in hot water is usually enough to keep the food bowls nice and clean. Don't use soaps or any other type of household cleaners when you are cleaning your food bowls.

Water Fresh and Salt

Your Hermit Crabs are also going to need a healthy amount of fresh and salt water in order to survive. Some species of Hermit Crabs like to submerge themselves in water. If you plan on using a deeper bowl for their water, make sure you give them a way to climb out because most water dishes are far too smooth. So what do you do? I place an authentic Sea Sponge in mine. This gives them a perfect way to climb out when they want to. You could also use a small piece of drift wood.

Using a Sea Sponge also introduces a possible problem. Sea Sponges that are constantly wet are the perfect place for mold growth. If you choose to use a Sea Sponge, it will have to be cleaned on a regular basis.

A Sea Sponge will also help you regulate and keep humidity levels where they should be. I'll talk a little more on that later.

Should You Use Fresh Water from the Tap?
The simple answer to this question is, no. Most tap water is heavily chlorinated. I prefer to use bottled water that has no chlorine. You can get a one gallon jug at the local super market for around $1.00. One gallon of fresh water will last you quite a while!

If you don't want to purchase clean fresh water, you can purchase a water conditioner from the local pet store or your favorite online super store. Here are a couple of the more popular water conditioners on the market.

• Tetra BettaSafe Water Conditioner
• API Tap Water Conditioner
• Tetra AquaSafe PLUS Water Treatment
• Zoo Med ReptiSafe Instant Terrarium Water Conditioner

Each one of these products should provide plenty of instruction on how to rid your tap water of any potentially damaging contaminants. I still think it is much easier to buy spring water from the local grocery store.

Your Hermit Crabs Need Salt Water Too!
Hermit Crabs are naturally found in tropical environments that are typically surrounded by salt water. If you don't provide your Hermit Crabs with salt water, then they will die. Not only do Hermit Crabs like to drink salt water, it is also very helpful during a molt, something I will talk about a little later.

Preparing Salt Water for your Hermit Crabs
Don't even think about using ordinary table salt. It is not even an option here. The salt we use on our food is not the same as the salt that is found in the ocean. You are going to need to purchase salt that is made specifically for salt water aquariums.

There is one brand that comes highly recommended from salt water aquarium enthusiasts and it is called: Instant Ocean Salt. You can find it at most pet stores and online. Amazon carries small 10 gallon containers that will last you a very long time.

I don't recommend other brands because some of them add extra chemicals that can harm your Hermit Crabs.

You will find all the information you need on mixing the salt on the package. Just remember to use de-chlorinated water and you won't have any issues.

You should also check their water bowls every morning to make sure they still have plenty of water. It won't hurt to change their water every morning either. This is a great way to prevent mold growth. Just wipe the water bowls with a clean paper towel, refill them and your Hermit Crabs will be happy!

Maintaining Proper Humidity Levels

Keeping humidity levels where they need to be is pretty easy. I've already told you that you should purchase a temperature / humidity gauge. In order for your Hermit Crabs to live out a healthy and happy life, you are going to need to make sure the humidity levels in their habitat are a constant **75-80%.** Your humidity gauge will tell you if you have reached the magic number, but how do you maintain a constant humidity level in the habitat? A simple spray / mist bottle will do the trick!

Fill a small misting bottle with clean chlorine free water and lightly mist the inside of the habitat. If you live in a dry part of the world, then you will need to do this quite often. You can overdo it too! Too much water will cause mold growth. You don't want this.

Just lightly mist the habitat and keep an eye on the humidity gauge. The humidity gauge doesn't really update in real time so you might have to check back to see what the "actual" humidity levels are. Once you get a feel for this, it is really easy to maintain the correct humidity levels no matter where you live.

If you find that you are having trouble keeping humidity levels where they are supposed to be, you may want to think about keeping a damp Sea Sponge in the habitat, but keep an eye on the sponge because it might start to get moldy. Mold and Hermit Crabs don't mix.

Cleaning the Habitat

It won't take very long to figure out that Hermit Crabs are messy little creatures. If you are the type of person who likes everything to remain in one place all nice and tidy, your Hermit Crabs are going to drive you nuts.

These little creatures don't care for any sort of organization. You might think you have found the perfect place to place their food dish. The Hermit Crabs will think otherwise and move it. They will also move just about anything you place inside the habitat. If they "can" move it. They will! Which brings us to the cleaning phase.

Yes, you will need to clean your Hermit Crab Habitat at least once a week

No, It is not difficult!

If you maintain the proper humidity, remove leftover food every morning, locate the little hidden stashes of food your hoarding Hermit Crabs hide and clean out their water dishes you won't have too much to worry about when it comes time to clean the habitat.

While we are on the topic of "**cleaning**," the actual "**cleaning**" part should never consist of using any type of store bought soaps or cleaners. Most modern cleaning products have enough chemicals in them to quickly kill your entire Hermit Crab army. You have been warned. Don't use them.

The Hermit Crab Habitat Clean Up Process
The first step in properly cleaning your Hermit Crab habitat is removing all of your Hermit Crabs. They will only get in the way of your cleaning. This is where an additional isolation tank comes in handy. If you have one, then gently place all of your Hermit Crabs in the isolation tank and let the cleaning fun begin!

While you are at it. This is also a good time to make sure you still have all of your Hermit Crabs. They do climb and they will escape if you have forgotten to properly secure the lid of their habitat. You may also have a Hermit Crab who has buried itself because it is time to molt. I'll cover that topic a little later.

Remove Everything from the Habitat

Start by removing everything from the habitat. This includes water dishes, food dishes, hideouts, toys, shells and climbing toys. Once you have everything removed, you can get a much better understanding of what your Hermit Crabs are leaving behind.

If you are using Sea Sponges, now is a good time to let them dry out and letting them dry out is the single best way to keep them clean and free of mold. If you live in a hot climate, a few hours in the sun will do the trick. If you don't have that luxury, then you will need to purchase another sponge while this one dries out. The only way to get a Sea Sponge completely clean is by letting it dry completely!

Once everything is removed from the habitat, look for any type of debris and remove it. If you have chosen to use coconut fiber as your substrate, inspect the substrate for mold, bugs or food. Remove and replace any that seems dirty or ruined.

The same goes for any other substrate. You might need to remove the top layer and replace as necessary.

Take a close look at any other items you may keep in the habitat. Things like driftwood, hideouts and empty shells are going to need to be inspected too! Typically these things don't get too dirty and don't need to be cleaned, but if you feel that they do need a cleaning never use soap or store bought cleaners. I have found hot water to be the best cleaner!

Once you are satisfied, it is time to put everything back where it belongs. Don't worry about putting everything exactly where it was because your Hermit Crabs won't seem to notice. They may even like it if you rearrange their habitat.

Deep Cleaning

If you are cleaning your Hermit Crab habitat on a weekly basis, then a "deep clean" won't be necessary all that often. Some successful Hermit Crab owners don't ever do a deep clean. I like to schedule a deep cleaning every other month. It is a fairly simple process much like a regular cleaning, but I go one step further by cleaning or replacing the substrate.

Money Saving Tip!

If you are using play sand as part of your substrate, then you can simply sift through the sand and remove any type of debris or clumps you find. If you live in a warm and sunny part of the world, you can place the play sand in the sun for a few hours to help sanitize and clean it. If you don't have that luxury, then you will need to place the sand in an oven at about 150°C (300°F) for around a half an hour.

LET THE SAND COOL BEFORE PLACING IT BACK IN THE HABITAT!

Once the sand has properly cooled, put everything back together and let your Hermit Crabs explore

Bath Time!

I bet you didn't think you would be giving your Hermit Crabs a bath, did you? Well, you don't **have** to give them a bath but they sure do seem to enjoy it! Here's what you need to do. Remember the golden Hermit Crab rule here.

Don't Use Tap Water!

I have already mentioned this but it is worth mentioning again. Don't use tap water in any part of your Hermit Crab habitat.

How Do You Prepare the Hermit Crab Bath Water?

Much like human skin, a Hermit Crab's exoskeleton can dry out. You don't want this to happen. I like to use an additive for my Hermit Crab's bath water. The additive is called Stress Coat and the brand name is API.

This particular product contains Aloe Vera. This is a plant with great natural moisturizing capabilities. This will help keep your Hermit Crabs from drying out. Read the instructions on the label to determine how much Stress Coat you should be adding to your Hermit Crab's bath water.

Water Temperature is Important

Pay close attention to the bath water temperature. If the water is too hot, you may accidentally cook your Hermit Crabs. You don't want to do this. If the water is too cold, it will also hurt your Hermit Crabs. The water temperature should be "tepid" or just slightly warm to the touch.

The actual bathing process is really simple. Place a small amount of bath water in a container. Make sure that it is not too deep. You don't want to actually submerge your Hermit Crabs. You just want enough water for them to walk around in.

Place your Hermit Crabs in the water upside down so that the shell is the first thing to touch the water, not their feet. This will give them the opportunity to slowly come out of their shell and start exploring the bathtub. It will also help clean their little legs and pincers without filling their shells with water.

Let them wander around in the water for a few minutes but don't put them back in the habitat until they are dry. If you put them back wet, they will get covered with substrate and the whole bath would have been pointless.

Some Hermit Crabs will come completely out of their shells and clean themselves in the bath water. This is normal.

How Do You Dry Your Hermit Crabs?
Don't get any silly ideas about using a hair dryer to dry out your Hermit Crabs. This is not a good idea. The best and simplest way to dry out your Hermit Crabs is by simply placing them in a dry container that is lined with paper towels. Let them run around on the paper towels for a few minutes and they will be dry enough to place back into the habitat.

The Molting Process

Hermit Crabs go through an interesting process when they start to grow. Unlike us, they simply can't go to the store and buy new clothes. They have to actually shed or "molt" their entire exoskeleton. The exoskeleton is not the shell they crawl into. The exoskeleton is the entire outside of their body. I'm talking about that hard colorful shell that covers their legs, pincers and everything else. This is their exoskeleton and in order to properly grow, the old exoskeleton must come off!

Don't Panic!

I still remember the first time my son's Hermit Crab molted. My son came running into the run with eyes full of tears and yelled, "Dad, Purple Pincher is dead! He is dead!" "Purple Pincher" was the name my son chose for his Hermit Crab. Oh know, I thought to myself. I quickly made my way to the Hermit Crab habitat and sure enough, our little Purple Pincher appeared to be dead. He wasn't moving and he was no longer wearing his shiny little shell he always hid in. I knew what was going on but my son was freaking out.

I calmed him down and explained the situation. I told him that in a few days, Purple Pincher would be bigger, stronger and prettier than ever.

Signs of Molting

Some Hermit Crabs show signs that they are about to molt. They generally become slow and lethargic. Some will even attempt to bury themselves. If you can get close enough, you may even notice a slight milky or cloudy color to their eyes. This is normal, but you do need to protect your molting crab from the habitat if you have more than one Hermit Crab. Some Hermit Crabs will eat a molting Hermit Crab. Yes, you read that correctly. Your cute little Hermit Crabs can be cannibalistic.

Protective Barrier

If you know exactly where your molting Hermit Crab has buried itself, then you can easily provide it with a wall of protection. Cut a one or two liter bottle in half. The top half of the bottle makes the perfect protective barrier. Just gently place the larger opening around the buried Hermit Crab and slowly move it in small circles until it touches the bottom of the habitat. Leave the top of the bottle open to allow good airflow.

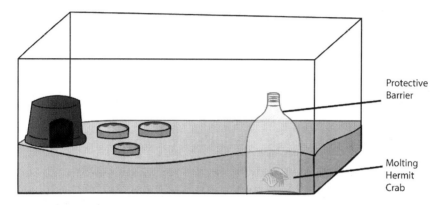

Protective Barrier

Molting Hermit Crab

Isolation Tanks
Some people prefer to move their molting Hermit Crabs to an isolation tank. This can be very stressful for the Hermit Crab. I don't really recommend this, but if you prefer this method here's what you need to do.

The tank should be setup the same. You need to make sure you have plenty of substrate. You need to make sure the temperature is correct and you need to make sure the humidity levels are between 70-80%.

What Should You Do When Your Hermit Crab is Molting?
This is the easy part because molting is a perfectly natural process and once you have isolated your Hermit Crab, it is best to sit back and let nature take its course. If your Hermit Crab has decided to bury itself during the Molting Process, then all you need to do is mist the ground where it has been buried. Don't mist your Hermit Crab if it has decided to molt above ground. Just leave it alone until the process is complete, but be ready to provide plenty of food once the Hermit Crab is finished because it will be very hungry!

How Long Does Molting Last?
The molting process seems to vary for each Hermit Crab. Some Hermit Crabs will take as little as a week to molt while others may take as long as four months. You might find yourself wanting to check on your Hermit Crab once it has started molting. Don't do this. You will do more harm than good. Just be patient and wait it out.

The molting process is very stressful for Hermit Crabs and some don't live through it. If your Hermit Crab has died, it will usually smell pretty bad in the isolation tank.

The time it takes your Hermit Crabs to molt will generally depend on the size of the individual crab. Larger crabs usually take much longer to molt. Smaller crabs are generally much quicker.

Benefits of Molting
When your Hermit Crab has finished the molting process, they will look shiny and new. If your Hermit Crab lost a leg in a fight, you may notice the lost leg has reappeared. You will also notice your Hermit Crab seems more colorful. Their exoskeleton is brand new! It should look it. You may also notice that the tips of their legs are now very, very sharp! Without the molting process, your Hermit Crabs would never be able to grow.

What To Do After the Molt?
I have already said this, but the molting process is very stressful for your Hermit Crabs. When the actual molting process has completed, your Hermit Crab will not be able to move at all. They need a few days for their shiny new exoskeleton to harden. Again, leave them alone.

When they emerge from the ground, remove the protective barrier and be ready to provide them with plenty of fresh food and water. If you chose to use an isolation tank, you can keep them in the isolation tank for a few days as long as they have plenty of food and water.

If you happen to see your Hermit Crab's old exoskeleton, leave it alone. If they haven't already, your Hermit Crab will eat it. It is an excellent source of nutrients and it will help them replenish their strength.

Common Problems and What to Do About Them

In a perfect world there would be no need for this portion of the book, but problems can and will happen. Knowing how to respond to these problems will make them much easier to manage should they arise.

Losing Legs
When Hermit Crabs are really stressed out, they lose their legs. They just fall off. This can seem a little scary at first. **Don't panic.** Stress is the cause. If you notice this happening when you first bring your Hermit Crabs home, then the stress of the move is likely the culprit.

If your Hermit Crabs are losing their legs after they have already established a healthy lifestyle in their habitat, then something is wrong in the habitat.

Check the habitat temperature. **The temperature needs to be 70-75 degrees Fahrenheit or 21 to 23 degrees Celsius.**

Check the humidity levels in the habitat. **The humidity level should be 75-80%.**

Fighting
Don't panic! There is a chance a couple of your Hermit Crabs will fight. This is completely natural but some fights can turn ugly really quick. It is not uncommon for Hermit Crabs to lose legs or pincers during a fight. Don't worry because they will grow back during the next molt.

If you happen to notice that one particular Hermit Crab seems to be acting like a bully, then you may have to remove it from the habitat. Keep your eyes on the bully and don't let it continue to bully the other Hermit Crabs.

Shell fighting is also a common scenario in the habitat. This happens when one Hermit Crab sees another Hermit Crab in a shell that it wants really badly. The Hermit Crab might even climb on top of the other Hermit Crab and start rocking the shell back and forth until the Hermit Crab leaves.

If you made sure to provide plenty of extra shells, then you shouldn't have too many shell fights.

Shell Less Hermit Crabs

There are instances when a Hermit Crab will decide to leave its shell and run around the habitat completely naked. This isn't good because it leaves the Hermit Crab extremely vulnerable. **Don't panic!** If one of your Hermit Crabs is doing this, it is best to place it in an isolation tank with plenty of empty shells. This will encourage the naked Hermit Crab to find a home.

Insects or Pests

Any type of insect inside the habitat is a problem, but **don't panic**. If some of your Hermit Crabs like to hide food, or you missed some while doing your morning clean up routine, then the food could be the source of the problem.

The easiest way to fix this problem is by cleaning the entire habitat from top to bottom. I would even go so far as replacing all of the substrate. Once you have cleaned the habitat, give all of your Hermit Crabs a bath.

Mold

Again, don't panic. Mold can be caused by two different things. The most common cause of mold in a Hermit Crab habitat is too much humidity. Check your humidity levels and ensure they stay in the 75-80% range.

Mold can also be caused by not removing old food from the habitat. Keep the habitat clean and you won't have any mold problems.

Noise

Some Hermit Crabs make chirping sounds. **Don't panic.** This is perfectly natural.

Death

Death is a natural part of life. Hermit Crabs don't live forever. It can be hard to lose one of your Hermit Crabs, but don't let that stop you from enjoying the good times with your little friends. Whenever one of our Hermit Crabs dies, we bury it in the yard.

Thanks!

Thank you for picking up a copy of my book. I really do appreciate it. I would like to ask a favor. Can you PLEASE leave a review of my book on Amazon? It really helps other Hermit Crab owners locate my book.

I would love to hear about your Hermit Crab army. Drop me an email if you feel like sharing a story or two and don't hesitate to send over an email if you have any questions. I will do my best to lend a helping hand. You can email me at:

wordsaremything@gmail.com

Made in the USA
Lexington, KY
14 February 2018